THE  COOKBOOK

The simple way to get your greens

DAWN RUSSELL

To Jamie, Alexander, Leo
and Rosie

CONTENTS

8Greens
for
A HEALTHY
LIFE

This book is for everyone who has found it impossible or unpleasant to get enough greens into their daily lives. If you are too busy for complicated preparation, don't want unrecognizable or horrible-tasting food, or have children who think they hate this stuff, I get it. I faced all those challenges, along with two even bigger ones: I barely knew how to cook and had just left hospital.

When I was 25 I was diagnosed with stage III (out of IV) cancer. I contracted a bone infection during my fourth surgery that left my immune system too compromised to receive radio- or chemotherapy. This left me facing a life-threatening illness with

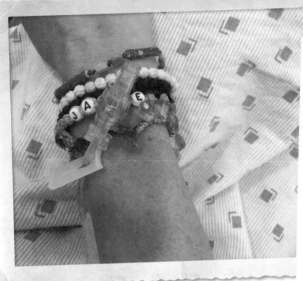

nothing more traditional medicine could offer. I spent four years researching and trying integrative therapies such as Chinese tonics, acupuncture, yoga, vitamin C injections, Indian cleansing rituals, menthol gauze wraps, light therapy and so on. I went to every "must see" doctor, lost count of the centers around the world I visited, and top universities' trial studies I leapt at. When you are desperate, you try everything.

Little did I know after these years of searching I'd end up back in my West Village apartment in New York starting with the basics of food. Being so ill, it was evident the effects food had on my body. Strawberries? I broke out in a rash. Mushrooms? I could not keep them down. Greens were the first thing to get me to 10am without requiring a nap. My kitchen looked like a farmers' market crossed with a health food store and science lab – blenders with sticky notes taped everywhere, and bottles of supplements marked with instructions all over them.

I was very fortunate: I ended up healthy, on the Board of Beth Israel's Hospital for Integrative Medicine in New York, and convinced that a large part of my recovery, and continued health, was thanks to the changes I had made in what I ate. Especially the daily addition of eight green ingredients: spinach, kale, blue-green algae, spirulina, chlorella, barley grass, wheatgrass and aloe vera.

But now I had a family who were far from convinced that they had to eat this stuff too. I was married to a man who refused to have the green drink I made every day with these ingredients, had small children equally suspicious of "healthy food", and was surrounded by friends with little idea of what specific greens could do for them, or how to include them in a busy family life. It became clear that even with all the green juices and powders on the market, something else was needed. It took five years of trial and error to get these eight green ingredients from farms into an effervescent tablet that could just be dropped into a glass of water – a drink that actually tasted good, didn't take hours to prepare, and that didn't contain any sugar. During those years my husband tasted 263 different blends as we worked to get it right; my family dealt with a lot of glasses of green liquid on the kitchen counter. In 2015 8Greens was launched and sold 2 million tablets in its first year.

Making 8Greens meant I spent a lot of time with these ingredients, and these tablets, in my kitchen. I had a growing family and an endless procession of meals; and often

2000
Aged 25, Dawn Russell diagnosed with stage III (of IV) cancer

2001
Dawn begins her research into complementary medicines

2003
Dawn joins the board of Beth Israel Hospital's Center for Integrative Medicine as a patient advocate and voice of experience

2008
Estée Lauder supports Dawn's foundation, funding outreach to schools, universities and hospitals

2007
Dawn joins Donna Karan in establishing the Urban Zen health initiative

2005
Dawn Russell Foundation is established to be an advocacy and mobilization campaign to increase young women's health

2010
Development of 8Greens begins: what are the most important greens for human health? How can they be made to fit into real life in a way that is easy and tastes great?

2012–14
Dawn sets out to find the best raw materials suppliers for her 8Greens. She visits farms, lakes and factories to ensure the best. The greens go through a simple process of dehydration with no enzymatic or chemical breakdown of the ingredients

8Greens ingredients are sourced from CGMP-compliant, HACCP-compliant, Kosher- and Organic-certified suppliers. 8Greens is blended to exacting standards in a GMP-certified facility that is registered and audited by the DFA's Therapeutic Goods Administration

MANUFACTURED IN THE USA

2015
5 years of testing,
5 manufacturers,
263 prototypes later,
8Greens is created

talked with other parents about the challenges of making greens that didn't take ages to prepare, tasted good, and that everyone wanted to eat. I started to find new ways of introducing 8Greens into my family's mealtimes, creating and adapting our favorite recipes. My husband and boys loved them so much I started to make them for friends, who suggested I share them. The result is this cookbook. Every recipe has passed the key criteria of being made by me (this means you definitely can), containing eight green ingredients, and being eaten with enthusiasm by all at the table. You will even find a chapter on cocktails that are improved by the addition of 8Greens: we all need to unwind a little too, and healthier is a bonus.

I believe that changing my nutrition changed my health, and I developed 8Greens to help everyone prioritize their nutrition no matter how hectic their lives. 91% of Americans don't eat the recommended daily intake of green vegetables. This is a combination of the challenge of time, budget and the perception most of us picked up as kids that greens don't taste good. It really doesn't have to be this way. I had no choice but to get healthy, but my efforts to help my family do the same had to fit into normal life and satisfy normal taste buds. I hope you and your family like these recipes too.

SPINACH

Alkalizing properties help support a healthy aging process

Rich in anti-oxidants, vitamin A, calcium, iron

SPIRULINA

Assists in supporting a healthy digestive system and digesting sugar

Assists with the body's natural ability to lose weight

8Greens INGREDIENTS

BLUE-GREEN ALGAE

Assists with weight loss and stress

Boosts immune system, energy, memory, metabolism

BARLEY GRASS

Promotes a healthy immune and digestive system

Contains thousands of active enzymes and naturally-occurring chlorophyll

ALOE VERA

Promotes the natural healing process

Soothes stomach irritations,
promotes immunity

WHEATGRASS

Rich in alkalizing minerals

Supports healthy red blood cell
production

Supports healthy circulation and
fights inflammation

CHLORELLA

Supports the body's natural ability to
remove toxins

Rich in amino acids

KALE

Seven times more beta-carotene
than broccoli

One of the healthiest vegetables
around, giving maximum nutrition

STARTERS

8 soups

8Greens Spinach soup

We all know the importance of spinach – think of Popeye's muscles. But the taste of soggy boiled spinach leaves put me off for life. This recipe changed that. This is a soup my family loves so much we cheers our mugs before drinking.

Serves 3–4

Ingredients

1½ teaspoons olive oil

½ large onion, chopped

1 garlic clove, crushed

½ teaspoon paprika

¼ teaspoon ground cumin

1 cup spinach leaves, washed

1 8Greens tablet
dissolved in 3 cups stock

Method

Heat olive oil in pan over medium heat, sauté onion for 4 minutes until softened.

Add garlic, paprika, and cumin, tip in spinach and cover pan with a lid. Cook for 5 minutes, until spinach is wilted.

Transfer everything to a high-powered blender, add hot 8Greens stock, blend.

Serve hot.

The most important fact about **onions** is that 75% of their nutrients are found in the top two layers. **Red onions** are oh-so-slightly more nutrient-rich than white onions. Red onions are better used in dishes such as salads, while white onions are sweeter, milder and are great for adding flavor to cooked dishes such as this one.

8Greens Butternut squash soup

For a sweeter palate. That would be me…

Serves 4

Ingredients

1 large butternut squash, unpeeled and cut into cubes

1 large onion, chopped

1 cup cherry tomatoes

3 garlic cloves, peeled

1 tablespoon extra-virgin olive oil

½ teaspoon Himalayan salt

1 8Greens tablet dissolved in 2 cups chicken or vegetable stock

Method

Preheat oven to 320°F.

Put all vegetables in a large bowl, pour over oil and season with salt. Using your hands, mix everything so that all vegetables are well coated with oil.

Scatter vegetables over baking tray, roast in oven for 45 minutes until skin of butternut chunks is very soft.

Transfer vegetables to a high-powered blender with 8Greens stock and blend until smooth.

Serve hot.

The health benefits of **squash** range from helping with sleeplessness to supporting prenatal health. Being an anti-inflammatory and anti-oxidant, squash helps reduce breathlessness, boosts respiratory health and supports good gut health.

Squash is among the oldest cultivated crops on earth originating 10,000 years ago in Mesoamerica – one of the "Three Sisters Crops" that were cultivated by Native Americans and eventually shared with European settlers, making squash a staple of early American cultures' diet.

SQUASH:
HIGH IN
VITAMIN A
BETA-CAROTENE
GOOD FOR
EYE HEALTH
SKIN HEALTH
STRONG BONES

Be Well × 8Greens Broccoli soup

Celebrity nutritionist Kelly LeVeque has actually cracked the code to making a tasty broccoli soup with all the added 8Greens nutrients.

Serves 4

Ingredients

4 cups broccoli florets

1 cup peeled and chopped white root vegetables (I like parsnip, turnip and white potato)

4 tablespoons olive oil

2 tablespoons ghee or grass-fed unsalted butter

3 garlic cloves, minced

1 small shallot or ¼ cup yellow onion, chopped

1 teaspoon thyme leaves

1 teaspoon oregano leaves

1 teaspoon parsley leaves

1 8Greens tablet dissolved in 1 quart chicken bone broth (or use vegetable broth)

2 cups spinach leaves

½–1 teaspoon Himalayan salt (optional)

Optional toppings

2 tablespoons ghee or grass-fed unsalted butter

2 tablespoons chopped shallot

1 kale leaf, sliced

4 fresh sage leaves

Olive oil or coconut milk

Red pepper flakes

Method

Preheat oven to 350°F.

Scatter broccoli florets and root vegetable chunks on a baking tray, drizzle with olive oil, mix by hand to coat with olive oil. Roast in oven for 20 minutes, flipping halfway through so they caramelize but don't burn.

Meanwhile, in a large pot, melt ghee or butter over a medium–low heat. Add minced garlic and shallot or onion, sweat for 4–5 minutes, turn heat down to low. Stir in thyme, oregano and parsley until shallot is soft and translucent.

When broccoli and root vegetables are done, add 8Greens broth to pot, raise heat and bring to a rolling boil. Tip in roasted vegetables and cook for 10 minutes.

Off the heat, add spinach to soup, stirring in leaves with spoon. Transfer to high-powered blender, blend. Taste and add salt, if you wish.

If you want to add toppings, in a small pan heat ghee or butter over a medium-high heat and sauté shallot, kale and sage leaves until crispy.

Serve soup warm, topped with crispy shallots, kale and sage leaves. Or simply drizzle with olive oil or coconut milk and scatter with red pepper flakes.

8Greens Chicken noodle soup

Who doesn't need hot chicken noodle soup when they are ill, cold or feeling the general winter blues? It is like a big hug from mama.

Serves 4

Ingredients

2 teaspoons coconut oil

2 cups leftover cooked chicken, shredded

½ cup sweetcorn (canned or fresh)

⅔ cup frozen peas

2 carrots, thinly sliced

3 celery stalks, thinly sliced

1 8Greens tablet dissolved in 5 cups chicken stock

1 teaspoon smoked paprika

Himalayan salt, to taste

⅔ cup dry clear rice noodles

Method

Melt coconut oil in a large pan, then add all ingredients except noodles.

Simmer over low heat until vegetables have softened. Add dried noodles, then simmer until soft.

Serve hot.

Stock – beef, chicken, fish, etc – is a mega healing food that most mommies and doctors prescribe for those under-the-weather because bone broths are nutrient-dense, easy to digest and boost healing. Chicken stock in particular contains amino acids that help first thin and then expel mucus in the lungs. Our ancestors used every part of the animal, boiling and simmering marrow, skin, feet, ligaments etc. for days. While it may sound horrid, the simmering releases health compounds like collagen, glycine and glutamine that have endless benefits including healing the gut, protecting joints, supporting immunity, promoting metabolism, protecting against food intolerance etc.

8Greens Mint, pea & spinach soup

Serves 4

Ingredients

Olive oil, for sautéing

1 onion, chopped

1 8Greens tablet and 2 vegetable stock cubes dissolved in 4 cups water

1¼ cups frozen peas

1¼ cups fresh spinach

2 tablespoons omega oil

2 mint sprigs, leaves picked and chopped

Himalayan salt, to taste

Method

Heat olive oil in pan over medium heat, sauté onion for 4 minutes until softened.

Pour in 8Greens stock, add peas and spinach, cook for 5 minutes.

Add omega oil and chopped mint and cook for another 3 minutes.

Transfer soup to high-powered blender, blend until smooth. Add salt to taste.

Serve hot.

Peas assist with weight loss, are a blood sugar regulator and are anti-aging and anti-carcinogenic.

8Greens Kale green soup

Kale is a nutrient-dense superfood which has seven times more beta-carotene than broccoli. The ancient Greeks domesticated it 2,500 years ago, and no doubt mothers have despaired of getting their children to eat it for 2,499. But if you or your family think you don't like kale, this soup should change your mind...

See page 14 for photo of finished dish

Serves 4

Ingredients

Olive oil, for sautéing

2 large leeks, chopped and washed

3 cups washed and finely chopped kale

1 cup washed and finely chopped spinach

1 cup orange lentils

3 teaspoons chicken or vegetable stock powder

1 8Greens tablet dissolved in 5 cups water

Method

Heat olive oil in a pan, sauté leeks for 10 minutes over a medium heat, stirring occasionally.

Once leeks have softened, add kale, cook for 5 more minutes.

Add spinach, cook for another 5 minutes.

Tip in lentils, cook for another 5 minutes.

Add powder stock to 8Greens water, pour into pan and simmer for up to 1 hour over a low heat.

Serve hot.

LEEKS ARE
ANTI-BACTERIAL
ANTI-VIRAL
ANTI-FUNGAL
ANTI-OXIDANT
ANTI-CARCINOGENIC

Kale has zero fat, is low in calories but high in fiber. It is the top lutein-containing food, which is known to be good for eye health

8Greens Zucchini soup

Serves 4

Ingredients

Olive oil, for sautéing

½ onion, chopped

1 garlic clove, chopped

2 zucchini, diced

2 little potatoes, diced

2 cups vegetable or chicken stock
(fresh or made from a cube)

1 8Greens tablet dissolved
in ½ cup water

3 tablespoons omega oil

2 tablespoons probiotic powder

Method

Heat the olive oil in a pan, sauté onion and garlic until softened.

Add zucchini and potato chunks, pour over stock and 8Greens water to cover vegetables. Bring to boil, simmer until vegetables are soft.

Add omega oil and probiotic powder, transfer to high-powered blender and blend to your preferred consistency.

Garlic is a great cough and cold remedy, reduces risk of stomach or colon cancer and makes you less attractive to ticks.

Zucchini is a type of squash that contains vitamins C and A and fiber. It is a favorite to aid weight loss as it is low in calories, carbs and sugars but high in nutrients.

8Greens Tomato soup

The greatest tomato tip I learned was from Rosie: balsamic vinegar kills tomatoes' extreme acidity and adds a little sweetness. But there's no need for it in this tomato soup. My kids drink this in their school flasks during the chilly months.

Serves 3

Ingredients

1 tablespoon olive oil

2 medium onions, chopped

5 cups ripe cherry tomatoes, cut in half

1 **8Greens tablet** dissolved in 2 cups chicken stock

1 medium sweet potato (leave skin on but wash before dicing)

½ teaspoon Himalayan salt, to taste

1 tablespoon omega oil

Method

Heat olive oil in pan over medium heat, sauté onions for 4 minutes until softened.

Add tomatoes and cook for 10 minutes until softened.

Pour in 8Greens stock, increase heat to high and bring to boil. Once boiling, add sweet potato and simmer until soft.

Take pan off heat, add omega oil. Transfer soup to high-powered blender and blend until smooth.

Season with salt and serve hot.

When cooking **tomatoes**, keep the seeds in the recipe as they contain invaluable nutrients. Ideally use the whole tomato, skin and all, to get highest level of lycopene, which is amazing for skin and hair. Avoid aluminum cookware as the high acidity of tomatoes may interact with the metal.

TIPS FOR KIDS

1 Sneak in more fiber by adding flaxseed. I shake some on top of their morning cereal. The seeds act as a natural laxative, and are also one of the reasons my kids' hair and nails grow like weeds.

After steaming vegetables use the leftover water in a smoothie. All the nutrients and minerals are stored in this water so it makes a great booster to any drink.

3 Give kids little to no orange juice as it is sooooo mucus-producing. My baby was very ill at infancy and the doctor instructed us to stop orange juice to help clear his chest and lungs.

4 The great Linda McCartney has an amazing frozen burger for those mommy-in-a-pinch moments.

5 Lemon kills mucus so try a little squeeze of lemon on food when they have colds.

6 Sneak in omega oil every day in their food to give them strong nails, hair and skin. Moms always ask about my kids' hair.

7 A Brazilian doctor told me to take 1 teaspoon of manuka honey (try for UMF+20) every morning; now my kids have no colds or mucus build-up. Costly but worth it.

8 Sneak in probiotic powder any and everywhere. There are great childrens probiotic powders but get the most billion live culture you can find. Probiotics are good bacteria that keep a gut healthy. We are only as healthy as our gut...

DAILY GUIDELINES

(Just that – *guidelines*. Not to be exactly executed every day
or they will become unmanageable, and you utterly miserable)

A.M.	LUNCH	4PM	DINNER
Eggs	Barley	Snacks	Protein
Muesli	Rice	(see page 90)	Vegetables
Yogurt	Beans	e.g. Almonds,	(also the time
Smoothie	Soup	Toast, Honey,	of day for glass
	Bread	Banana, Berries,	of wine or other
	Salad	Yogurt, Smoothie	drink, if that's
			your thing)

BREAKFAST

Eggs twice a week. I simply can not do egg whites, but for those who can, well done. I love poached, my boys love boiled eggs with soldiers (a Brit invention – you dip strips of hot buttered toast into a soft-boiled egg), and my husband is an old school scrambled egg type of guy.

Any smoothie in this book is great for breakfast, and of course muesli, granola or oatmeal (but always check labels for sugar levels).

LUNCH

Improve your carbohydrate intake by including lentils, brown rice or quinoa at lunchtime.

A Russell favorite is brown rice, quinoa or lentils, black or red beans, with vegetables and **Rosie's red sauce** (page 52). Or do **Mom's chili** (page 44) or **Lentils of Spain** (page 43).

Any vegetable will do: broccoli, zucchini, green beans, sugar snap peas, spinach, carrots...

Any **soup** (pages 16–31) makes a good lunch with some gluten-free bread, or some salad with an 8Greens **dressing** (pages 80–89).

DINNER

Increase protein intake by including red meats, such as grass-fed beef or lamb in your diet. Try a **marinade**, like ours on page 50, maybe served with **ratatouille** (page 46).

Russell dinnertime favorites are **Gwyneth's fish fingers** (page 48) and **meatballs** (page 54).

We love fish – salmon, sea bass, cod – or chicken, with **pesto dressing** (page 86) or **ratatouille** (page 46) on top.

Any gluten-free pasta (never white pasta) with **pesto sauce** (page 86) or **Rosie's red sauce** (page 52).

Vegetables: broccoli, rocket, green beans, cauliflower, sugar snap peas, spinach, carrots...

... and in that mommy pinch, Linda McCartney burgers.

8

MAIN DISHES

Nanny Jenny Salmon

Nanny Jenny was Alexander's beloved maternity nanny. She had every trick up her sleeve, not only with babies, but with domesticity as well. I felt Nanny Jenny took my hand and walked me into mommy-hood, and domesticity.

Serves 3

Ingredients

1lb 2oz salmon fillet

1 8Greens tablet
dissolved in ½ cup water

Juice of 1 lemon

½ teaspoon Himalayan salt

Dill or your favorite herb, to taste
(optional – I find children
do not like herbs)

Method

Preheat oven to 350°F.

Place salmon fillets in baking dish and pour over 8Greens water, lemon juice, salt and herbs, if using.

Bake in oven for 20 minutes until salmon is cooked through and no longer pink.

**SALMON
IS THE GOD
FOR GOOD SKIN**

Lentils of Spain

This dish comes directly from a magical *finca* in Spain where I hounded the poor cook until I got this versatile recipe.

See page 38 for photo of finished dish

Serves 6

Ingredients

2 tablespoons olive oil

1 small onion, chopped

1 garlic clove, crushed

1 large carrot, grated

1 red bell pepper, deseeded and sliced

1 green bell pepper, deseeded and sliced

1¼ cups red split pea lentils, soaked in cold water overnight then drained

1 8Greens tablet dissolved in 4 cups water

3 teaspoons powder stock

½ teaspoon paprika

1 cup passata

Method

Heat olive oil in pan over medium heat, sauté onion, garlic, carrot, and peppers until softened. Add lentils, sauté for 5 more minutes.

Dissolve the powder stock into the 8Greens water. Add to the lentils along with paprika and passata, turn down heat to low and simmer until lentils are soft. This takes about 20 minutes.

Mom's Chili

I know there is no chili in this chili, but that is my mom.
She beats to her own drum and this recipe is fantastic on
a cold day.

Serves 4–6

Ingredients

¼ cup olive oil

4 cups lean ground beef

2 large yellow onions, chopped

2 teaspoons ground cumin

2 teaspoons dried oregano

2 cups canned whole tomatoes

1 carrot, grated

1 zucchini, chopped

1 small can red kidney beans
(about ⅔ cup), drained

1 8Greens tablet dissolved
in 2 cups vegetable stock

1 small can tomato paste
(about ⅔ cup)

Splash of balsamic vinegar
(cuts acidity of tomato)

2 tablespoons chopped garlic

1 teaspoon cayenne pepper

2 tablespoons omega oil

Himalayan salt and pepper,
to taste

Method

Add half the olive oil to a pan over a medium–high heat
and fry beef until browned and cooked through.

Remove beef from pan using a slotted spoon to drain off
liquid; set aside. Pour away liquid.

Add remaining oil to pan and sauté onions until soft.
Add cumin and oregano.

Cut tomatoes into big chunks and add to pan with their
juice, grated carrot and chopped zucchini. Add seasoning
to taste, simmer for 20 minutes.

Add beef and beans with 8Greens stock, tomato paste,
balsamic vinegar, garlic and cayenne and simmer for
1 hour with no lid.

Add omega oil and serve.

Kidney beans are high in protein and high in
fiber. Red is the most commonly used type of
this bean as the firm coat is better for slow-
cooked dishes. White kidney beans are more
subtle in flavor and are better in salads or
dishes that have only a little cook time.

GREAT FOR
HAIR &
SKIN HEALTH

8Greens Ratatouille

Serve as a main course or as a side dish with meat or fish.

Serves 2–4

Ingredients

2 tablespoons olive oil

1 medium red onion, sliced

1 red bell pepper,
  deseeded and sliced

1 green bell pepper,
  deseeded and sliced

3 large tomatoes, chopped

3 zucchini, sliced

3 garlic cloves, chopped

1 tablespoon omega oil

1 8Greens tablet
  dissolved in ½ cup water

Method

Heat olive oil in pan over medium heat, sauté onion until softened.

Add peppers and lightly sauté for a few minutes.

Add all other ingredients and simmer until zucchini is cooked through and slightly softened but still has some bite.

Bell peppers are high in fiber, anti-oxidants and vitamin C. Green peppers have a bitter taste because they spend less time on the plant and are also cheaper than the brighter-colored versions. When given more time to ripen, peppers become red or yellow and are sweeter and more fruity in taste. **Red peppers** contain 11 times more cancer-fighting beta-carotene than green.

Gwyneth's Fish fingers

Gwyneth Paltrow absolutely nailed this fish finger recipe. My boys love them. I am married to an Englishman who has a cultural attachment to the frozen fish fingers he grew up on at school, but which I find weirdly industrial. Gwyneth's keep our whole family happy, as they taste great and are made from healthy ingredients. Not easy.

Serves 4

Ingredients

4 white fish fillets, cut into fingers

3 garlic cloves, sliced

Juice of 1 lemon

1 tablespoon chopped parsley

1 cup gluten-free breadcrumbs

1½ teaspoons dried oregano

1 teaspoon dried garlic powder

1 teaspoon fine Himalayan salt

1 8Greens tablet
   dissolved in 1 cup soy milk

2 tablespoons olive oil

Lemon wedges, to serve

FISH:
FULL OF
OMEGA-3s
GOOD FOR
HEART
CIRCULATION
JOINTS
EYES
LUNGS
SKIN
CONSTIPATION
& BRAINS

Method

The night before, place fish fillets in a baking dish with garlic, lemon, and parsley. Cover and marinate in refrigerator overnight.

The next day, preheat oven to 450°F.

Stir together breadcrumbs, oregano, garlic and salt and tip onto a plate.

Remove fish fillets from marinade and shake off excess marinade, dip fillets into the 8Greens/soy milk mixture. Once dipped, roll fish fillets in breadcrumb mixture to evenly coat.

Lay coated fish fingers on baking tray and lightly drip both sides with olive oil. Bake in oven for 10 minutes until brown and crispy.

Serve with lemon wedges.

8Greens Marinade for any red meat

The purpose of this cookbook is to show that almost any meal, any recipe, or any drink can get added nutrients from 8Greens. This 8Greens marinade does the same for meat. How easy is that?

Serves 2

Ingredients

2 garlic cloves, crushed

1 teaspoon finely grated ginger

2 teaspoons soy sauce

Juice of 1 small lemon

1 teaspoon runny honey

1 8Greens tablet dissolved
in 2 tablespoons water

1 fresh chili, chopped (optional)
(If you like it extra hot, like my
husband, leave the seeds in...
you have been warned).

Method

Combine all ingredients in a bowl. Spread over red meat to coat.

Leave for at least 1 hour to marinate. For best flavor, leave to marinate overnight.

What are the key benefits of 8Greens?

// I hope the biggest benefit of 8Greens is that is makes these greens accessible for anyone. What puts a lot of people off including these greens in their diet is a combination of the effort, the cost, the time to prepare them and their taste. A tube of 8Greens can be wherever you or your kids are. It is affordable, and it gives you all these greens in a drink that tastes really good. It really does: this is why it took me and my husband five years and 263 different versions to get it right. //

Rosie's **8Greens** Red sauce

Since Rosie arrived in our household no food has or will ever taste as good in my home. Friends ask for "the Rosie invite."

Rosie's red sauce is great with pasta, meatballs, chicken – literally anything. Rosie is Italian, need I say more? It is my three-year-old's third-favorite thing in life. First being his brother, second being chocolate.

Serves 4–6

Ingredients

1 tablespoon olive oil

2 medium onions, chopped

3 garlic cloves, crushed

2 bay leaves

1 teaspoon dried oregano

4 cups cherry tomatoes, cut in half

1 teaspoon balsamic vinegar

Himalayan salt, to taste

1 8Greens tablet dissolved in 2 tablespoons water

¼ cup chopped basil leaves

Method

Heat olive oil in a pan over medium heat and sauté onions until softened.

Add garlic, bay leaves and oregano. Add tomato halves, balsamic vinegar, salt, and 8Greens water. Turn down heat to low and simmer for 45 minutes until sauce has reduced and thickened.

Remove bay leaves and add chopped basil. Pour everything into a high-powered bender and combine until smooth.

Gwyneth's Turkey meatballs

My boys love to help roll and make the meatballs. However, it can quickly become a sticky mess so please put a little olive oil on the tips of their fingers to prevent a total kitchen disaster.

Serves 4

Ingredients

1 beaten egg

1 **8Greens tablet** dissolved in 2 tablespoons almond milk

2–3 slices gluten-free bread

4 cups turkey mince – or fresh salmon mince

½ onion, finely chopped

½ zucchini, grated or finely chopped

1 corn on the cob, kernels sliced off

½ teaspoon garlic powder

½ teaspoon Himalayan salt

2 medium tomatoes, chopped

Gluten-free flour, for dusting

Olive oil, for frying

Method

Stir together beaten egg and 8Greens milk in a shallow bowl. Add bread slices, turn them around to coat, then leave to soak for a minute or two until bread has softened.

Mix all remaining ingredients except tomatoes together and add soaked bread. Stir everything together until combined, then shape into small balls. Place balls into a bowl of gluten-free flour and roll them around to coat.

Put a little olive oil into a large pan over medium heat and fry meatballs for 10 minutes until browned.

Add chopped tomatoes and cook slowly for 45 minutes until tomatoes have broken down into a thick sauce.

MAPLE SYRUP

HONEY

XYLITOL

DATES

STEVIA DROPS

VANILLA

PRUNE SYRUP

ALTERNATIVES TO ~~SUGAR~~

MAPLE SYRUP

A natural alternative to sugar that is high in anti-oxidants, nutrients and minerals such as potassium, magnesium, iron and zinc. Maple syrup is derived directly from the sap of maple trees, whereas refined cane sugar goes through a complex process to be condensed into crystallized sugar. Maple tree syrup, or sap, has been used for centuries. Sap from various maple trees first started being processed into syrup long before European settlers even arrived in America. Native Americans celebrated the Sugar Moon (the first full moon of spring) with a Maple Dance and viewed maple sap as a source of energy and nutrition.

The glycemic index score of maple syrup is 54 (compared to 65 for cane sugar). This means that maple syrup nutrition impacts blood sugar levels less drastically than table sugar.

PRUNE SYRUP

Apologies, but it is part of life... amazing for constipation and safe to dilute in water and give to babies. Babies often struggle with constipation when switching from breast milk to formula or to solid food. Prune syrup is heavy and dark and we use it primarily for baking.

DATES

For centuries dates have been referred to within the Islamic tradition as beneficial to pregnant women. The Journal of Obstetrics and Gynecology in 2011 investigated this ancient belief. The results were: improved cervical dilation, fewer damage to membranes, fewer drugs required, shorter labors:

"It is concluded that the consumption of date fruit in the last 4 weeks before labor significantly reduced the need for induction and augmentation of labor, and produced a more favorable, but non-significant, delivery outcome."

Top-quality dates are hand-picked directly from the fruit bunch and sold unprocessed, but most commercial dates are harvested by cutting the entire cluster which is then fumigated, cleaned, graded, packed and stored under refrigeration before being sold.

Dates are commonly used for preparing drinks, chopped in salads or savory dishes and – if soft – eaten directly.

XYLITOL

This is a natural sweetener from the fibrous parts of plants. It does not break down like sugar and can help keep a neutral pH level in the mouth, preventing bacteria from sticking to the teeth.

There is much debate that xylitol derived from birch bark is superior to xylitol from corn (actually the corn cob, not the kernel). But birch-bark xylitol means harvesting bark from birch trees, so save a tree and go corn cob.

VANILLA

Vanilla is derived from orchids of the *Vanilla* genus which bear pods ranging in size from 5-22cm in length – the larger the size the higher the value. Harvesting pods is labor- and time-intensive since they need to be hand-picked at a precise time to ensure the pods do not pop. Commonly available forms of vanilla include extract, paste, powder and whole pods.

Vanilla has always been and remains one of the most trusted remedies in natural healing. Natural vanilla extract contains numerous anti-oxidants, anti-inflammatories and anti-bacterials that assist in preventing acne and promoting digestion.

STEVIA

This is a plant grown in Brazil and Paraguay since the 16th century, when indigenous peoples used the plant to sweeten drinks and medicines. The word "stevia" refers to the entire plant; "steviol glycosides" is the sweet component purified from the leaves. It is a naturally-occurring, zero-calorie sweetener.

In 2008 the FDA declared stevia safe in foods and beverages. Clinical studies proved steviol glycosides (meeting purity criteria established by the JECFA) have no effect on blood pressure or blood glucose response, indicating stevia sweeteners are safe for diabetics. Based on the wealth of published research and independent scientific experts in both the US and globally, stevia sweeteners are safe for people of all ages, populations and an Acceptable Daily Intake (ADI) of 4 milligrams per kilogram body weight has been established. I prefer stevia in liquid form as it is more concentrated and goes directly into drink or food.

HONEY

To make one pound of honey, 60,000 bees must travel to 2 million flowers (around 55,000 miles) to extract enough nectar. Wow, that is dedication. Thank you, bees.

One tablespoon of honey is 64 calories and has no fat or cholesterol. The ancient Greeks, Romans and Egyptians documented honey's healing properties: Aristotle mentions it as early as 384 BC, and in the Bible, King Solomon said:

"My son, eat thou honey, for it is good."

Honey includes vitamins, enzymes, amino acids and minerals like calcium, iron, sodium chlorine, magnesium, phosphate, and potassium. Because of its acidic pH level (3.2–4.5) and anti-oxidant properties, it helps support a healthy immune system to protect against disease, radiation, bacteria, mold, fungi and viruses. Honey has been shown to support healthy blood sugar levels, promote natural healing and reduce gastric and throat issues.

Manuka Honey

My second son was very ill as a baby. I saw a leading Brazilian doctor who told me: "This is not cure but prevention. Give both your boys a teaspoon of the highest number manuka honey every morning for general health." I have done so every day since and they reap the benefits.

Manuka honey, produced in New Zealand by bees that pollinate the Manuka bush, is one of the most beneficial forms of honey in the world. Its nutritional content is up to four times that of normal flower honeys.

Genuine UMF Manuka Honey

The minimum UMF rating recognized is UMF5, however, it is not considered beneficial unless it carries a UMF 10+ level of antibacterial activity in the honey. Anything ranging from UMF10-15 is useful; anything UMF16 and up is considered superior quality.

The genuine product will have a UMF trademark clearly labelled on the front of the container; it will be from a New Zealand UMF-licensed company and labelled in New Zealand with the UMF company's name and license number on the label, as well as a UMF rating number.

HAVE YOU HAD YOUR 8G TODAY?

cilantro

$3.00/ bunch

BASIL

ARUGULA

$4/bunch

DAIRY

With endless contradictory advice on dairy, it comes down to personal choice. For me, dairy is a good way to get live culture probiotics. High acid levels in the stomach and bile in the small intestine can lead to the death of healthy gut bacteria. Some probiotic bacteria are more resistant than others, making consumption of probiotics with food, including milk, yogurt and other dairy products very beneficial.

The dream is to make it yourself...
good luck. I buy ready-made

Homemade is always the dream, but it is also unrealistic to consistently find both effort and time. Store-bought kefir usually contains 7–9 strains of probiotic yeast and bacteria, whereas homemade kefir can contain more than 50. Store brands are pasteurized after the fermentation process to extend shelf-life. This pasteurization limits the life of beneficial microbes. Having said all that, I made it once, gave up, went to the market and have bought it ever since.

Regardless of whether it's homemade or store-bought, Kefir is a mega-powerful probiotic, far more powerful than yogurt. It has been proven to inhibit the growth of various harmful bacteria. It contains high levels of vitamin B12, calcium, vitamin K2, biotin, folate, enzymes and probiotics. *The Journal of Dairy Science* published a study that discovered that kefir helps stop breast cancer growth; *The Journal of Immunology* found it has positive effects on allergies and asthma and *The Journal of Osteoporosis International* found that consuming kefir increases bone density and reduces risk of osteoporosis. All this means any kefir is better than none, even if it is store-bought.

The good and the bad

The good news is that soy can protect against breast cancer and its recurrence. It can also help relieve symptoms of menopause, can reduce the risk of osteoporosis and may protect against other forms of cancer, like endometrial cancer.

The bad news is how the isoflavones in soy affect hormones. This can disrupt estrogen-sensitive systems in the body, including the reproductive system, brain and pituitary gland. You decide.

My go-to milk

Coconut milk is often considered a "miracle milk" since it has the ability to support the body's immune defences, improve digestion, relieve constipation, provide electrolytes and reduce fatigue. Sounds great, but remember that, because of coconut milk's high saturated fat content, it should be consumed in moderation.

Amazing skin results if you can handle the taste... I can not

Because goat milk has a pH level similar to humans, it's absorbed by the skin with less irritation and helps eliminate skin bacteria (a nice way of saying acne).The fatty acids and triglycerides in goat milk are hugely beneficial, both inside and outside the body. Goat milk has high levels of vitamin A, which improves complexion, while the lactic acid in goat milk helps rid the body of dead skin cells and brightens skin tone.

Low in fat, but high in energy, protein, lipids and fiber

Almond milk is a good alternative to dairy products as it is high in anti-oxidants, vitamins, omega oils and necessary minerals. Almond milk has been a milk substitute since the Middle Ages, preferred over cow's milk for its long shelf life.The health benefits are its impact on weight loss, bone and muscle strength, blood pressure and kidney health.

PROBIOTIC (but kefir is #1)

Yogurt is possibly the most popular probiotic food. But not all yogurts are created equal.
Below is all you need to know:

BEST: raw yogurt from sheep or goats that are grass-fed, cultured 24 hours

SECOND BEST: organic yogurt from grass-fed animals

NOT GOOD: conventional yogurt (yes, this includes Greek yogurt)

REALLY NOT GOOD (the worst, in fact): sweetened conventional yogurt

The famous fruit cobbler

This dish is the first thing I cooked that my friends wanted me to share the secret with them. Every friend asks for this recipe, truly every one...

It began long ago when my surgeon at Memorial Sloan Kettering named me Ms. Cookie Monster because of my sweet tooth (more like sweet teeth). At a very serious, no-nonsense, disciplined, non-forgiving medical center, I was given this recipe to curb my sweet tooth, and thank you doctors, because we love it.

Serves 4

Ingredients

Whatever different fruits you like: blueberries, raspberries, strawberries, ripe mangoes, peaches, mandarins, passion fruits, pineapple, blackberries (5–6 cups chopped fruit for an 11 × 9 inch pan)

1 8Greens tablet dissolved in ¼ cup water

¼ cup coconut sugar or xylitol

1 cup gluten-free flour

¾ cup rolled oats

½ cup shredded coconut

1 tablespoon ground cinnamon

½ cup melted butter

1 tablespoon manuka +20 honey

Method

Preheat oven to 400°F.

Chop bigger fruits into bite-size pieces. We like to mix a few different fruits together. Add the 8Greens water and coconut sugar or xylitol to the fruit which will have a bit of liquid from the fruits.

Mix the dry ingredients in bowl, then stir in the butter and honey.

Cover bottom of a baking pan with the fruit, sprinkle cobbler topping over.

Bake in oven for 15 minutes or until top is golden. Serve hot or cold.

Peninsula Hotel Beverley Hills Pancakes

I could not be more excited to introduce you to these pancakes. They're the Russell household's hands-down favorite pancake, and it took us a few years of being loyal Peninsula Hotel guests to win over the super-lovely James Overbaugh to get his personal recipe which he developed over many years while trying to perfect a healthy pancake for himself.

Makes 16 pancakes to serve 4

Ingredients

2 tablespoons ground flaxseed

⅓ cup barley flour

⅓ cup spelt flour

1 cup and 2 tablespoons gluten-free all-purpose unbleached flour

2 tablespoons baking soda

1½ teaspoons baking powder

1½ teaspoons Himalayan salt

2 tablespoons brown sugar

2 tablespoons apple sauce

1 tablespoon manuka +20 honey

3 large eggs, beaten

2½ cups low-fat buttermilk

2 tablespoons canola oil

1 cup rolled oats

1 8Greens tablet dissolved in 2 tablespoons water

Olive oil, for greasing

Blueberries

Maple syrup, to serve

Method

Add flaxseed, barley, spelt and all-purpose gluten-free flours to a large mixing bowl and thoroughly mix together. Add baking soda, baking powder and salt using a hand-held blender.

Add brown sugar, apple sauce, honey, eggs, buttermilk and canola oil and whisk to incorporate. Add rolled oats and mix until thoroughly distributed through batter, then stir in the 8Greens water.

Cook pancakes on a hot griddle or pan lightly coated with olive oil. Ladle ¼ cup batter onto griddle or pan. Sprinkle blueberries onto pancakes before batter sets.

Remove from pan and serve immediately with maple syrup. We like to dip the pancakes bite by bite into maple syrup so the syrup does not disappear into the pancakes. Also, this is a trick to use less syrup, which is certainly not something I tell my little ones.

Spelt flour is a relative of common wheat that, when left unrefined, contains approximately 17% protein, 9% dietary fiber and 3% heart-healthy fats.

8Greens Banana bread

I am a sharer of any and all health secrets that help us be our best with the least amount of work, but this recipe is a trade secret of the cook in a beautiful English castle who is extremely private about her recipes. This has been one of my husband Jamie's favorites since he was a child, I got him to do the asking, using his English diplomacy rather than my usual full-frontal New Yorker tactics.

See page 62 for photo of finished dish

Serves 4

Wet ingredients

3 extra-ripe bananas, mashed

¼ cup butter, melted – or you can sub for coconut oil, canola oil or vegan margarine

¼ cup maple syrup (the real stuff) or prune syrup

1 **8Greens tablet**
dissolved in ¼ cup water

2 teaspoons vanilla extract

2 eggs, beaten

Dry ingredients

1¼ cups gluten-free flour

2 teaspoons baking powder

1 teaspoon ground cinnamon

Method

Preheat oven to 350°F and grease a 2lb standard loaf pan.

In a medium-large mixing bowl, combine all wet ingredients. In a small bowl, combine dry ingredients Stir dry ingredients into wet mix until most of the lumps are gone, then pour batter into loaf pan.

Bake for 45 minutes or until a toothpick inserted into center of loaf comes out almost clean (the top should be golden).

Alternatively, you can make cupcakes by dividing batter among 12 paper cases in a muffin pan and baking for 15 minutes (use toothpick test to see if they need 5 more minutes).

Bananas help weight loss by having few calories, stabilizing blood sugar level, improving insulin levels, reducing bloating and reducing appetite by slowing stomach emptying. They provide good fuel to the body and reduce muscle cramping, making them an athlete's favorite. I think I might become a monkey.

Paleo **8Greens** Blueberry muffins

Paleo is an amazing way to eat; a diet full of nuts, meat, vegetables and fruits. One must avoid dairy, starches, sugars and alcohol, leaving it very tricky for most to adhere to long-term. Me included. So when my trainer gave me this paleo recipe, both my kids and I loved it. We add manuka honey for moistness. So much better than any store-bought muffin and so easy to make, I promise. I am kitchen challenged and I can make them in no time. A perfect Sunday activity with your kids.

Makes 12 muffins

Ingredients

3 eggs

1 8Greens tablet dissolved in ½ cup almond milk

3 tablespoons coconut oil

2 cups ground almonds

½ teaspoon vanilla extract

½ teaspoon baking powder

½ teaspoon baking soda

1 teaspoon ground cinnamon

1 cup blueberries (I use 1 cup in mixture and an extra ½ cup on top as we like a lot of blueberries)

Honey, to serve

Method

Preheat oven to 350°F.

In a large mixing bowl, using a hand-held blender, mix together eggs, 8Greens milk and coconut oil. Slowly stir in rest of ingredients until well combined. Divide mixture into a 12-hole muffin pan. I add more blueberries on top.

Bake in oven for 25 minutes.

Transfer muffins in pan to a wire rack to cool.

Once cool, remove from pan and drizzle honey on top for extra flavor. Serve.

Brownies, chocolate chip cookies, crêpes

Every chef will growl at this but it is called reality. Mommy needs cookies for tomorrow's school class, we are having friends over and need a quick dessert, my kids have an unexpected playdate, etc.

Add 8Greens nutrients to any pre-made brownie, cookie or pancake powders with half olive oil /half omega oil. Pretty good nutritional value for 5 minutes.

Serves 6–10

Ingredients

1 packet premade brownie/cookie mix

4 teaspoons omega oil

4 teaspoons olive oil

1 egg, beaten

1 **8Greens tablet** dissolved in ½ cup water

2 tablespoons probiotic powder

Method

Combine all ingredients in a large bowl and mix together well. Transfer mixture to a brownie pan (see the packet for size) or if making cookies, place on a baking sheet, spaced out, and bake in oven for 25 minutes. I like to underbake a little to keep them moist inside.

Transfer to a wire rack to cool in pan – I leave overnight to settle and harden.

No supermommy here – they do not exist.

I have lost count of the number of times I have quickly made these brownies in my pajamas for my son's class the next day.

And when my son asked Santa Claus his opinion, it was "delicious".

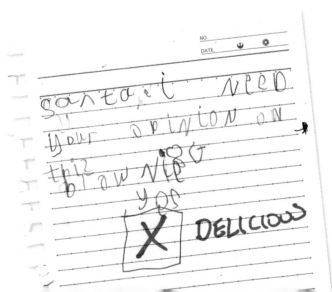

For crêpes

Thin pancake batter is essentially crêpes. Prepare the pancake batter mix following the packet instructions, adding the 8Greens water as above.

Ladle a little into the pan at a time, then cook one side of the crêpe and flip.

Add Nutella, which is basically hazelnuts (though kids think it's chocolate) to half the crêpe. Place sliced strawberries or bananas on top of Nutella. Flip in half and then quarter, then remove from pan.

If you are super-chefy, get a crêpe spreader to make a Sunday morning tradition of Nutella crêpes with the kids.

8Greens MAGIC

IT'S SO EASY TO SNEAK 8GREENS NUTRIENTS INTO ANY ULTIMATE CONVENIENCE BOX-MIX DESSERT

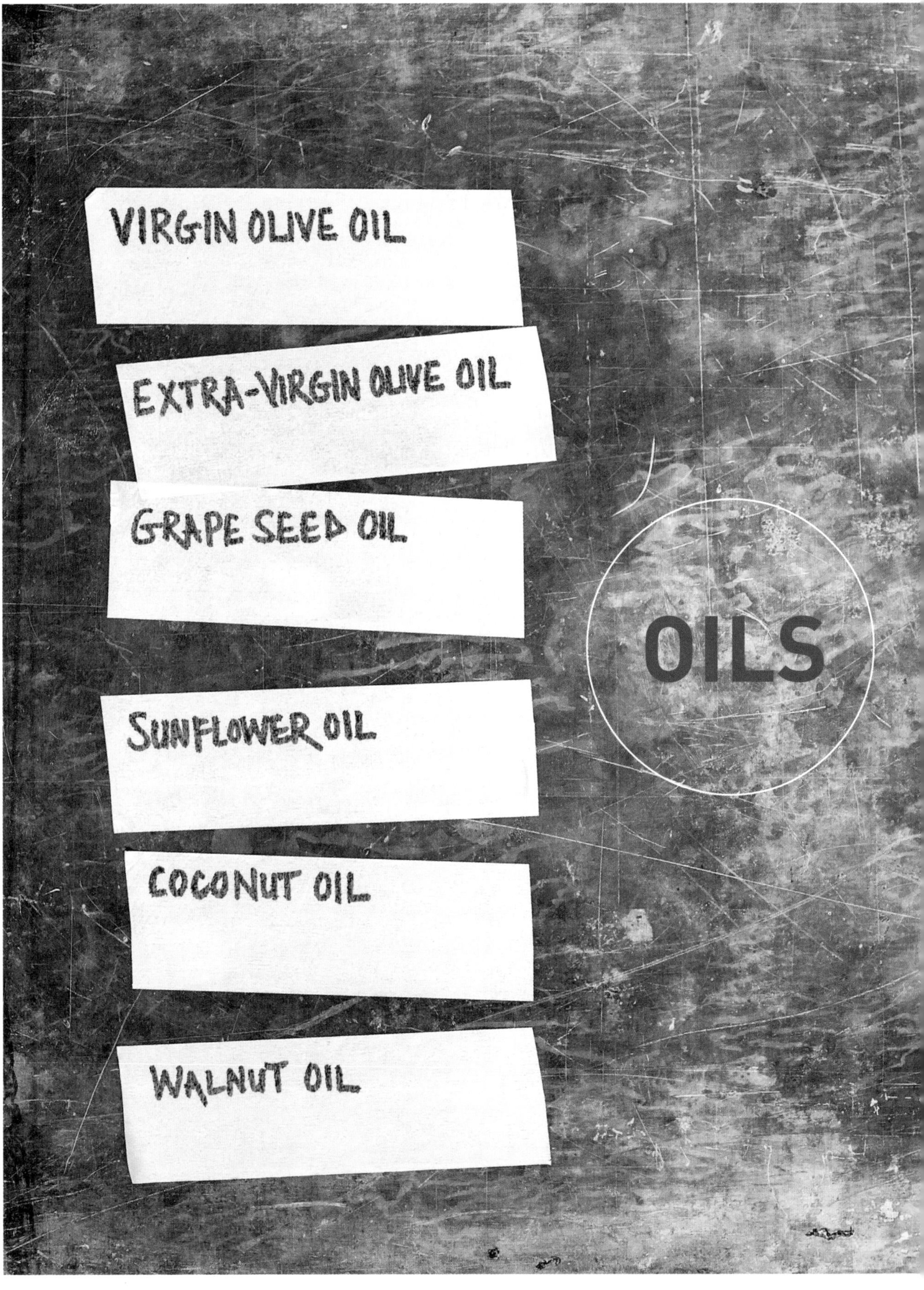

VIRGIN OLIVE OIL

EXTRA-VIRGIN OLIVE OIL

GRAPE SEED OIL

OILS

SUNFLOWER OIL

COCONUT OIL

WALNUT OIL

OLIVE OIL

Olive oil is the oil released when pressing whole olives. It is one of the healthiest edible oils since it contains fewer saturated fats, yet includes linoleic (omega-6) and linolenic acid (omega-3) essential fatty acids at a recommended 8:1 ratio, vitamins E and K.

Extra-virgin olive oil

This is the highest quality oil as it is not blended with other oils, has a lower level of oleic acid and contains the natural vitamins and minerals found in whole olives. It is best used for dipping and salad dressings as its flavor is damaged by heat.

Virgin olive oil

This is a "first press" oil but is blended with other oils. It has a lighter flavor with 2% acidity, as opposed to 1% in extra-virgin olive oil.

All olive oils have great benefits which are now commonly recognized:

Stimulates skin and hair growth

Helps regulate metabolism and reproductive system

It can be used as body lotion, make-up remover and eye cream... my kids find it hilarious when I dip my finger in it and rub it around my eyes after meals. Why not?

Soaking your nails in olive oil can strengthen them... I know this firsthand as after my second pregnancy my nails ripped a lot

SUNFLOWER OIL

Pressed from sunflower seeds, it is most commonly used for frying food, but the balance of fatty acids and high amounts of vitamin E, A, C and D found in sunflower oil means it is also used as an emollient in cosmetic formulations.

Sunflower oil is often used in infant products and eye creams as it's so gentle

It can be used as an acne moisturizer because the vitamins, fatty acids and anti-oxidants help regenerate skin while fighting acne-causing bacteria

GRAPESEED OIL

This oil can be controversial in that it is usually a by-product of wine-making. Once juice has been pressed from grapes for wine, oil is extracted from the crushed seeds. Regardless of being a by-product, grapeseed oil has huge beauty benefits, being rich with polyphenols, strong anti-oxidant compounds, polyunsaturated fats (PUFAs) such as omega-6 and omega-9, fatty acids and vitamin E.

Grapeseed oil's essential fatty acids performed well in clinical anti-wrinkle trials and have also proven to be effective at minimizing the prominence and size of scars

It has found its way into cosmetic products, especially those meant for the face and hair, as it is known to prevent acne and the signs of aging

FLAXSEED OIL

I swear by flaxseed oil. I sneak it into any- and everything to help skin, hair, digestion, constipation, tension, cancer prevention – its powers are endless. As it name suggests, it comes from the seeds of the flax plant. The seed is 40% oil by weight and of this 55% is omega-3 fatty acid. Discovering this truly, literally made my day. The health and beauty benefits of 55% omega-3 are endless. I and my children (full disclosure: not my husband) even do shots of it when feeling sluggish. I really can't say enough good about it.

COCONUT OIL

This is my go-to oil for its immense health benefits. It is an edible oil extracted from the kernel or meat of mature coconuts harvested from the coconut palm. Though high in calories – roughly 120 per tablespoon – coconut oil has great beauty benefits.

Coconut oil is used as skin moisturizer and make-up remover

It contains natural anti-bacterial and anti-fungal compounds

It's the absolute best dry hands moisturizer I have found

WALNUT OIL

Walnut oil is, as one would guess, extracted from walnuts and is made up of 64% polyunsaturated fatty acids, 23% monounsaturated fats and 9% saturated fats and contains no cholesterol.
It's used less often in food preparation as it needs to be diluted by half because of its super-strong flavor. We love it over vegetables, meat or in salad dressings, as it has huge amounts of omega-3.6.9, giving big, big beauty benefits.

Walnut oil has an undesirable greasy texture but with regular application helps diminish fine lines and wrinkles

It's the answer to horrible fungal infections that can really do your head in

It can fight dandruff and remove all dirt in scalp... great for kids

Add walnut oil to salads to help make you feel full and fight craving

I sneak it in my kids food as it helps ensure a good night's sleep since it contains melatonin; you have to be sneaky as it is a challenging taste for kids

How do you want people to use 8Greens?

"I want it to become just a part of daily life. The way one buys face cream, toothpaste and underwear – simply part of every day. These greens are a vital part of strong internal health, but their inconvenience, cost and taste has put most people off including them in their life. 8Greens set out to change this, and to makes these greens an easy, tasty and affordable part of everyone's routine."

8g GARLIC BAY
DRESSING

8g HONEY
MUSTARD
DRESSING

8g MINT
DRESSING

8g BALSAMIC
DRESSING

8
DRESSINGS

8G PESTO

BE WELL GREEN 8G DRESSING

8G ASIAN DRESSING

8G DILL DRESSING

I have tried to include a dressing that works with almost any food: salads, vegetables, legumes, meats, poultry, fish and fruit. Dressings are a great way to make a lot of healthy food taste more varied, interesting or just better (for kids and grown-ups); plus they are good ways to get really healthy oils into our diets. 8Greens works really well in dressings and is an easy way to boost the greens content without any extra chopping, blending or cleaning.

Be Well × **8Greens** Green dressing

Serves 8–10

Ingredients

1 8Greens tablet
  dissolved in 1 cup water
½ cup olive oil
¼ cup lemon juice
½ avocado
½ cup chopped flat-leaf parsley
3 tablespoons chopped chives
1 garlic clove, minced
¼ teaspoon Himalayan salt

Method
Put all ingredients into a high-powered blender
and combine until smooth.

GREAT over chopped vegetables.

8Greens Honey mustard dressing

Great for any salad. We like it on a robust, crunchy lettuce
like romaine or chicory – bitter leaves go really well with the
sweetness of honey mustard.

Serves 2

Ingredients

½ 8Greens tablet dissolved
  in 1 tablespoon water
1 teaspoon honey
1 teaspoon English mustard
Juice of ½ lemon
3 tablespoons extra-virgin olive oil
Himalayan salt and pepper,
  to taste

Method
Combine all ingredients in bowl and stir.

BRAIN
FOOD

Mustard is a good source of omega-3
fatty acids and helps with depression and
memory issues. Mustard can also relieve
pains and act as a laxative.

8Greens Mint dressing

Ingredients

½ 8Greens tablet
  dissolved in 1 tablespoon water

1 tablespoon cider vinegar

3 tablespoons extra-virgin olive oil

1 tablespoon finely chopped
  mint leaves

1 teaspoon honey

Pinch of Himalayan salt

Serves 2

Method

Put all ingredients into bowl and stir.

GREAT WITH coleslaw or as an alternative to mayonnaise.

8Greens Garlic bay dressing

Ingredients

½ 8Greens tablet
  dissolved in 1 tablespoon water

1 tablespoon red wine vinegar

3 tablespoons light olive oil

¼ teaspoon crushed garlic

2 bay leaves

Serves 2

Method

Put all ingredients into bowl and stir.

Remove bay leaves before serving.

DELICIOUS over green beans.

8Greens Dill dressing

Ingredients

½ 8Greens tablet
  dissolved in 1 tablespoon water

1 tablespoon cider vinegar

3 tablespoons light olive oil

1 tablespoon finely chopped dill

1 tablespoon stevia

Pinch of Himalayan salt

Serves 2

Method

Put all ingredients into bowl, stir.

AMAZING on cucumber salad.

8Greens Pesto sauce

Stored in an airtight container, this pesto can last up to three weeks in the refrigerator. We make it on a Sunday and throughout the week my boys ask for it on everything – salmon, chicken, pasta. It is a Russell staple.

Ingredients

¾ cup pine nuts

⅔ cup raw cashews

4 cups basil leaves

2 cups grated Parmesan

2 medium garlic cloves

⅔ cup olive oil

½ 8Greens tablet
   dissolved in ½ cup water

Serves 2

Method

Put all ingredients into a high-powered blender and combine.

Use immediately or store in the refrigerator.

8Greens Pesto dressing

Himalayan salt is a natural raw salt that contains far more trace minerals (84 at the last count) than industrial table salt (simply sodium chloride). It hugely detoxes the body and balances pH levels – this is important because acid is the killer which lowers immunity, weakens collagen, and is an all-round demon to health.

Ingredients

1 large tablespoon pesto sauce
   (see above)

2 tablespoons olive oil

1 tablespoon omega oil

Juice of ½ lemon

A pinch of Himalayan salt, to taste

Serves 2

Method

Put all ingredients in bowl and stir.

Add a pinch of Himalayan salt to taste.

Basil is referred to as the "holy herb".
It is anti-oxidant, anti-inflammatory,
anti-bacterial and fights against radiation.

8Greens Balsamic dressing

Serves 2

Ingredients

½ 8Greens tablet dissolved
  in 1 tablespoon water

1 tablespoon balsamic vinegar

3 tablespoons extra-virgin olive oil

Himalayan salt and pepper,
  to taste

Method

Combine all ingredients in bowl and stir.

GREAT WITH salad greens, bitter leaves like raddichio and treviso, tomatoes, grilled tuna...

Vinegar promotes weight loss, aids digestion and is a pain reliever as well as a great anti-oxidant.

8Greens Asian dressing

Serves 2

Ingredients

½ 8Greens tablet dissolved
  in 1 tablespoon water

Juice of ½ lime

3 tablespoons nut or sunflower oil

Splash of toasted sesame oil

1 teaspoon honey

1 teaspoon soy sauce

½ teaspoon finely grated
  fresh ginger

Method

Combine all ingredients in bowl and stir.

TRY WITH crunchy grated or shredded vegetables or slaws served alongside an Asian-inspired noodle dish.

Lime assists with weight loss, skin care, digestion and constipation.

Ginger helps ease feelings of nausea, reduces inflammation, soothes coughs and relieves migraines.

SNACK RIGHT

This is my pick of all the tips on snacking I have collected from centers, doctors, nutritionists and leading health experts. I am a huge snacker so I gathered them all. If I could, I would have a sweet, pastry or some other bad food every hour – but that is obviously not an option. Sadly.

Hummus with carrots, celery sticks, cucumber, pepper sticks or sugar peas. Hummus comes from the chickpea bean which is high in fiber yet helps prevent overeating

Gluten/wheat-free **bread** with avocado, honey and banana (my personal favorite) or sugar-free jam. Jam can contain huge amounts of sugar. Always try to find sugar-free

Probiotic yogurt with fruit (goji berries, blueberries, raspberries — any dark fruit is best). Probiotics equal healthy gut.

Fruit like dates, pomegranates, chopped pink lady apples, tangerines, mango, peaches... all satisfy that sweet tooth

Finn crisps with hummus or mashed **avocado**, which is a very healthy fat

Organic raw almonds (not roasted) are close to a perfect food. They reduce hunger, promote weight loss, stabilize blood sugar levels and contain magnesium, vitamin E, fiber and good fats

Try **tahini** or **peanut butter** on celery, apple or crackers. Add honey on top for sweetness

Apple sauce with blueberries. I love apple sauce but check the sugar content. We buy sugar-free and add blueberries

On a summer's day, my boys always reach for **frozen bananas** – a great way to save over-ripe bananas. Tastes as good as an ice cream (according to my sceptical husband) but is just a frozen banana. Peel them, wrap them in clingfilm, then freeze

Everything here tastes great, and is healthy, but do remember that healthy does not mean calorie-free – lots of healthy foods like oils and nuts are highly calorific... but they are the right calories

IF YOU'RE FEELING REALLY CRAP

I travelled the world for years researching the best complementary treatments. I had the force of an illness behind me and the luxury of time and financial support. Most places I travelled to one can forget Michelin star cuisine, thread-count bedding, or scented candles with calming music. It is hard core. From the mountain-top hospital in Bhutan to a village in France, below is all I learned...

Chop **ginger** into anything and everything. It is anti-cancer, anti-inflammatory, anti-aging. The key is to keep the best nutrients so chop, do not peel.

Goji berries have become very popular because they are low calorie and fat-free, but high in fiber and anti-oxidants. Great for a snack, or keep frozen to throw in smoothies.

Turmeric's anti-cancer power is one of the most-repeated piece of advice in many countries. The taste is quite overpowering so add honey or stevia.

Onions are anti-cancer, antibiotic, anti-parasitic. Always keep the top two layers as 75% of its nutrients are found there.

We all know the power of **garlic**. I found it fascinating and helpful (for kissing my husband) that Japanese garlic does not smell.

Our pH alkaline level upon waking should be 6.7–7.5. Lower means too acidic, which is the devil for good health. To get your pH level up sprinkle **chlorophyll**, **spirulina**, **wheatgrass**, **cilantro** and **cayenne** in your salad.

There are mega nutrients in **alfalfa**, **celery** and **cucumber** so throw some in the salad.

An important goal, which I achieve half the time, is for every meal to include **raw food**, because the enzymes break down for better digestion.

CHEW, CHEW, CHEW

That's the Mayo Clinic's mantra. For food to get to the blood system, we have to chew, otherwise it becomes a rock, there is no nutrition and we become bloated and it hurts. Additionally pH levels go down in cooked food so we need raw to keep our pH high.

DRINKS

8 for everyone

8Greens Original shake

Serves 4

Ingredients

1 cup almond milk

1 big cup ice
(2 cups for more of a shake)

2 tablespoons omega oil

1 tablespoon flaxseed

1 8Greens tablet
dissolved in 1 cup water

1 teaspoon vanilla extract

1 full tube of chlorophyll
(equal to about 20 drops)

2 tablespoons bee pollen

Method

Add all ingredients to a high-powered blender and combine.

Serve immediately.

**GOOD FOR
FATIGUE,
INFLAMMATION
CONSTIPATION**

Flaxseed is high in fiber, anti-oxidants and omega-3s for healthy heart maintenance.

Bee pollen is special: about half of its protein is in the form of free amino acids that are ready to be used directly by the body. It soothes dry skin, improves energy levels, decreases allergies, helps build the immune system and aids digestion.

8G ORIGINAL SHAKE

8Greens Morning tea

The best way to start the morning. For the full effect, ideally drink 30 minutes before eating – which I never do but always try to. 8Greens dissolves super-fast in hot water, which my kids love to watch as it looks like a volcano.

Serves 1

Ingredients

1 8Greens tablet dissolved in 1 mug (equal to 2 cups) hot water

2–4 tablespoons lemon juice (I do 4)

1 slice fresh ginger

1 teaspoon manuka honey

Method

Add all the ingredients to a mug and stir. I chew the ginger at end, as it has gotten soft by then.

Have you heard from people who use 8Greens?

// The best part of 8Greens for me is hearing from the people who love the product. Receiving emails and letters from mothers, jet-lagged executives, pro athletes and drained rock stars on tour is the most fantastic testament to all the hard work we put into creating 8Greens. As a mother, the feedback that means the most comes from other mothers. One mom wrote to 8Greens saying she goes to three schools a day with her kids, and that by the third she was always drained and irritable. Now she puts two 8Greens in her water bottle and feels she has way more energy and patience with her kids. Just yesterday one of our retailers came back from a European family holiday and said '8Greens made our trip'. In the past her kids and husband had been jet-lagged at the start of the day and crabby by the end of it, but this time she had heard none of that. Few things could make me happier than reading these stories. I made 8Greens so that anyone could have these greens in their diet in a way that fits real daily life. //

8Greens Anti-oxidant shake
= anti-aging... *skin, skin, skin*

Serves 4

Ingredients

½ cup natural yogurt

1 tablespoon probiotic powder

1½ cups blueberries

¼ cup orange juice
   (about 1 orange)

1 8Greens tablet
   dissolved in 1 cup water

Ice:
   (1 cup for a drink,
   2 cups for a shake)

Method

Add all ingredients to a high-powered blender and blend until combined.

Serve.

Oranges are high in vitamin C to promote the immune system and maintain the elasticity of the skin.

Blueberries are low in calories but high in nutrients. These anti-oxidant heroes reduce DNA damage, boost brain activity, support digestion and aid in weight loss.

8Greens Slimdown time

Drink before a meal as it will break down fat cells faster. This juice has a tangy taste and is my least favorite drink, but it works. Or you could do a "Heidi Klum" and take 2 tablespoons of apple cider vinegar before meals – too much even for me.

Serves 4

Ingredients

1 cup grapefruit juice
   (about 1 grapefruit)

2 teaspoons apple cider vinegar

1 8Greens tablet
   dissolved in 1 cup water

1 full tablespoon honey

2 cups ice

2 full tubes of stevia
   (equal to about 40 drops)

Method

Add all ingredients to a high-powered blender and blend until combined.

Serve.

Grapefruit is high in nutrients such as fiber, potassium, lycopene, vitamin C and choline to help maintain a healthy heart and boost the immune system.

Be Well × 8Greens Spa smoothie

Be Well is nutritionist Kelly LeVeque. While her list of Hollywood clients include Jessica Alba and Molly Sims, I was most interested in her because she understands the danger of sugar in our bodies. When you first see her, Kelly encourages clients to test their blood throughout the day, like diabetics, so they can better see their insulin swings.

Serves 1

Ingredients

1 8Greens tablet
   dissolved in 1 cup water

1 cup coconut milk

1 heaping tablespoon
   vanilla pea protein powder

¼ avocado

½ cup peeled and roughly chopped
   cucumber

2 tablespoons chia seeds

Juice of 1 lemon

1 cup ice

Method

Add all ingredients to a high-powered blender and blend until combined.

Serve.

Cucumber is rich in the two most basic elements needed for healthy digestion: water and fiber. The vitamins in cucumbers help ease anxiety and stress. Cucumber has anti-oxidant activity, a cleansing action against toxins and waste and a soothing effect on skin irritation. It also helps prevent constipation, improves hydration, protects against aging, reduces bad breath and fights inflammation.

86 BELL WELL SPA
SMOOTHIE

8Greens Reset smoothie

For tiredness, mood swings or a full reset. Perfect pre- or post-flight, to fight jet lag or to beat the 4pm slump.

Serves 2

Ingredients

1 **8Greens** tablet

1 cup coconut milk

1 cup frozen berries

¼ avocado

1 cup ice cubes

2 tablespoons chia seeds
(soaked in water overnight
for maximum benefit)

Method

Dissolve 8Greens tablet in coconut milk.

Add 8Greens coconut milk to a high-powered blender with all other ingredients; blend until combined.

Serve.

Coconut milk is good for healthy and strong teeth and nails. It makes a tasty alternative to dairy products and is high in essential vitamins and minerals such as magnesium and calcium.

Frozen berries are full of natural goodness and anti-oxidants – think skin.

Chia seeds are high in fiber, zinc and protein and are loaded with anti-oxidants to fight the production of free radicals.

Avocado is another ingredient that's great for your skin as well as for constipation, is full of omega acids and essential fatty acids to restore and repair the body and provides essential daily nutrients such as vitamin E, vitamin B6 and potassium.

8Greens Mint julep

A non-alcoholic version of the classic cocktail, with the added benefit of 8Greens.

Serves 4

Ingredients

5 mint sprigs, leaves picked

2 slices fresh ginger

1 8Greens tablet
   dissolved in 1 cup water
   (I like sparkling water)

1 full tube of stevia
   (equal to about 20 drops)

½ cup ice

Method

Add all ingredients to a high-powered blender and blend until combined.

Serve.

Mint is high in antibacterial properties and anti-oxidants to improve the immune system and aid digestion.

Ginger kick-starts digestion and relieves inflammation.

8Greens Lemonade

Perfect for detoxing, rebooting after poor eating or high intensity stress – which pretty much covers every morning for most of the world. Great drunk throughout the day.

Serves 1

Ingredients

1 8Greens tablet dissolved in 1 mug (equal to 2 cups) hot or sparkling water

2–4 tablespoons lemon juice (I do 4)

Sweetener of choice – try stevia, coconut sugar or maple syrup for their nutritional benefits, to taste

Method

Add all ingredients to a mug or glass and stir.

Serve.

Lemons are good for flushing out toxins, as well as balancing the digestive system. Great for improving the digestion and boosting the immune system, and for cleansing.

8
COCKTAILS

Being healthy and taking care of what we put into our body is very important. But constant perfection is an impossible goal: kicking back is just as important. With this in mind I teamed up with Juan Santa Cruz at Casa Cruz in London to see how we could use 8Greens to add some virtuous fizz to a few of my favorite cocktails. If you are looking for inspiration try the following at the end of a long week, or experiment for yourself.

Note: 8Greens takes longer to dissolve in anything other than water – just give it a little time.

8Greens Margarita

Serves 1

Ingredients

1 8Greens tablet

4 teaspoons lime juice

3 tablespoons tequila

4 teaspoons Cointreau
   or Triple Sec

Ice cubes

Salt, to serve

Method

Dissolve 8Greens tablet in lime juice, tequila and Cointreau or Triple Sec in a cocktail shaker. Shake well over ice cubes.

Strain into a chilled cocktail glass with a salted rim – use a Martini glass if straight up, small highball if on the rocks.

Why did you choose these 8 greens in particular?

// I lost count of how many greens I researched and tried. My recovery, and all my research showed me how important these particular greens were to internal health. When I was sick these were the greens that I noticed had the greatest impact on how I felt and my recovery. They were life-changing, and I do not say that lightly. I felt particularly strongly about blue-green algae (BGA). It's one of the most powerful greens there is, especially in terms of its anti-inflammatory properties (and so much of what we put in our bodies in Western industrial life inflames our system). It is the only 100% non man-manipulated green. It added a lot of complications and cost to making 8Greens, but I was adamant that it should be in there. Nearly all of the human-grade BGA available comes from one lake in the US, making it very hard to source and expensive, which along with its fragility is why it is in so few products. //

8Greens Aperol spritz

Serves 1

Ingredients

1 8Greens tablet

1 wine glass
  of Prosecco or Champagne

¼ cup Aperol

Ice cubes

Orange or lemon peel,
  to serve

Soda water, to serve (optional)

Method

Dissolve 8Greens tablet in Prosecco or Champagne.

Pour Aperol and 8Greens Prosecco or Champagne into a big wine glass full of ice, stir.

Add orange or lemon peel, and a splash of soda if you want it lighter.

8Greens Vodka soda fresh mint

Serves 1

Ingredients

1 8Greens tablet

⅔ cup soda water

¼ cup vodka

Mint sprigs

Lime juice, to taste

Method

Dissolve 8Greens tablet in the soda water.

Stir vodka and 8Greens soda water together over ice cubes and mint sprigs in a glass.

Add lime juice, stir, serve.

8Greens Pimm's

This is the most English of summer cocktails, and delicious on a hot day. It is super-easy to make, but also something you can make your own with what else you put in. Some people use ginger ale or champagne rather than lemonade, and the list of fruit you can add is endless. Either way 8Greens works so well because this is a drink you are meant to add to …

Serves 1

Ingredients

1 8Greens tablet

⅔ cup ginger ale

3 tablespoons Pimm's No.1

Ice cubes

Cucumber, apple and orange slices, and sprigs of mint, to serve

Method

Dissolve 8Greens tablet in ginger ale.

Pour Pimm's over ice cubes in a large glass, fill with 8Greens ginger ale.

Add a few slices of cucumber, apple and orange, and finish with a sprig of mint.

Stir, serve.

8Greens Tom Collins

Serves 1

Ingredients

1 8Greens tablet

⅔ cup soda water

4 teaspoons lemon juice

4 teaspoons sugar syrup

¼ cup gin

Lemon peel and cocktail cherry,
   to garnish

Method

Dissolve 8Greens tablet in soda water.

Stir lemon juice, sugar syrup and gin together over ice cubes in a glass (or mix in a cocktail shaker for a better result).

Top with 8Greens soda, garnish with lemon peel and cherry.

8Greens Bloody Mary

Serves 1

Ingredients

1 8Greens tablet

3 tablespoons vodka

1 teaspoon lemon juice

1 tablespoon Worcestershire
sauce

Pinch of celery salt

Pinch of ground pepper

Dash of tabasco sauce

½ cup tomato juice

Ice cubes

Celery stalk, olives and cherry
tomatoes, to serve

Method

Dissolve 8Greens tablet in vodka.

Stir all ingredients together well over ice cubes in
a glass.

Garnish with celery stalk, olives and cherry tomatoes –
whatever you prefer.

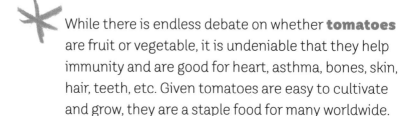

While there is endless debate on whether **tomatoes**
are fruit or vegetable, it is undeniable that they help
immunity and are good for heart, asthma, bones, skin,
hair, teeth, etc. Given tomatoes are easy to cultivate
and grow, they are a staple food for many worldwide.

8Greens Cruz 2.0

Serves 1

Ingredients

1 8Greens tablet

¼ cup ginger ale

2 tablespoons vodka

4 teaspoons apple liquor

1 passion fruit (fresh, purée
   or 4 teaspoons syrup)

Drizzle of ginger syrup
   or a little fresh peeled ginger
   and a spoon of sugar

Crushed ice, to serve

Method

Dissolve 8Greens tablet in ginger ale.

Pour all remaining ingredients into a cocktail shaker.
Shake well and strain into a glass full of crushed ice.

Add 8Greens ginger ale, stir, serve.

Passion fruit is considered a berry and despite its
small size, is a rich source of health benefits ranging
from cancer prevention, to improving skin health,
slowing signs of aging, assisting in sleep habits and
helping immune, digestion, bone, and eye health.
There are over 500 varieties and they can grow in
any climate without frost.

8Greens Caipirinha

Serves 1

Ingredients

1 8Greens tablet

¼ cup cachaça

4 teaspoons lime juice

1–2 sugar cubes
  or sweetener of your choice

Crushed ice, to serve

Soda water, to serve (optional)

Method

Dissolve the 8Greens tablet in the cachaça.

Put lime juice and sugar into a glass.

Pour in cachaça, and stir until sugar melts a little.

Fill with crushed ice, stir again.

To make it lighter, add a splash of soda water.

DAWN'S QUICK 911

⑧

EASY STEPS

BEST EASTERN

1 Chinese practices like acupuncture and cupping really work for me and were vital to my recovery. I have addressed both in more detail elsewhere, but please do engage with the important body of knowledge these practitioners employ and be open to the potential of things that may seem alien or counter-intuitiuve.

SUPERSOAK

2 Epsom salt baths are essential for me, and I have somehow become the spokesperson for Epsom Salts. While the bathtub is filling, dry brush your body as aggressively as you can. Use twice as much salt as recommended: not a cup but the whole bag. Experiment by adding a pound of baking soda to the bath. To dry off, just wrap a towel around you and lie on your bed to allow water to go into your skin.

SUPER SUPER SOAK

3 Once a month I pour a liter of apple cider vinegar into the bath. It is not fun at all but it is the best detox for my leg to keep working. If it can help my leg work, it can help anything.

THINK PINK

4 Always use Himalayan salt – this naturally occurring pink salt contains the same 84 trace minerals that are found in the human body, including calcium, potassium and magnesium to create electrolyte balance, increase hydration, improve circulation and alkalize the body.

WAKE UP CALL

5 If, like me, you have a compromised system and have mucus or congestion issues, in the morning add a teaspoon of baking soda and squeeze a lemon into a cup of hot water. Caution: do everything slowly or it will froth over the cup.

CLEAN TEA

6 Another amazing detox was given to me by an executive who constantly flies yet has skin of butter, and she is in her 60s. Drink dandelion tea every night before bed. It flushes out excess water, it is amazing for inflammation.

SWEET RELEASE

7 I love sweets, I mean love them. Glutamine supplements help sugar cravings. For real, I have used them.

KEEP IT REAL

8 I have seen so many think they are having a super-healthy breakfast by eating fat-free oatmeal. Read the label as there can be loads of hidden calories and added sugar.

ACUPUNCTURE

Acupuncture and cupping are so important for me because of the lack of circulation and sensation in my left leg. I had four surgeries to remove my lymph nodes, and many nerves were damaged in that area. Two glasses of wine and I need to do acupuncture the next day. Standing in heels at a wedding and I need to do cupping the next day. Otherwise, my leg becomes the size of a tree trunk and my foot will not fit into a shoe.

Westerners are still experimenting with acupuncture, whereas the Chinese have been using it for centuries. My Chinese acupuncturist speaks little English, has one dangling light bulb from a cracked ceiling in rooms that look alarming in terms of health and safety, but she is the real deal. She gets it and can explain the benefits to my body.

The theory behind acupuncture is its impact on the movement of energy through the body's meridians. The needles open up any blocks in the cycle of blood and energy flow in the body. The body's meridians contain *Yin* and *Yang*. The yang meridian goes down from our head to our feet, while the yin meridian runs from our feet up to our chest. The meridian flow keeps blood and energy moving through our organs. Acupuncture and cupping clear blockages that can accumulate in this system and so promote organ and general health. If this all sounds wacky to you, that's fine – just remember that when it comes to acupuncture increasing numbers of health insurers around the world approve it because standard data-driven and peer-reviewed studies have shown that it works in wide areas of human health.

I sent a friend to my Chinese lady. She called after to report "I can't take it, I don't know how you do it". A month later my friend was back. Because it worked.

I have, for better or worse, been to many places for treatment, detox, healing... My hope for this book is to distill my experience so that you, the reader, can decide what suits you. These are the only five centers I have to share from hundreds of centers and endless options of treatments or specialists. These are the ones that have had the most impact for me.

We Care Spa, California

Even though We Care Spa has become more commercial over the last 25 years of its life, it is still my annual stop. Which is saying something because I fly 11 hours, drive two more and leave my family for five days every year to go through this week of painful yet necessary detox. You cannot fault We Care for building upon their huge success and I do admire their lack of name-dropping visitors – from celebrities and CEOs to world leaders. I have yet to go without being with an A-list celebrity yet I love that no one cares. I do my own thing, but there are hourly classes to bond, learn and keep oneself busy.

It is not for the faint-hearted. You detox hardcore. You eat one cup of soup at 4pm, get daily colonics and take many supplements throughout the day. After my first visit, two decades ago, I found my own rhythm: arrive a day late, leave a day early and ask for a small smoothie and salad daily. I simply had to eat more. The treatments are some of the best I have had in the world. A massage where you can not even think or speak for hours after – that is rare.

As I have said earlier in the book, do not buy the whole program anywhere. Just get a few items and you can always buy more online. The process is not fun but the results are truly miraculous: I find their program really challenging, but go every year.

18000 Long Canyon Road, Desert Hot Springs, CA 92241, wecarespa.com

Mayo Clinic Executive Program

I know this is extreme both cost- and healthwise, but once in a lifetime it is a must. This is the state of the art of scientific medicine. I have never seen any other Western program like it. You utterly know your health for better or worse after, and are in a place where you can then get advice on whatever issues have been brought up.

200 First St. SW, Rochester, MN 55905, mayoclinic.org

Paracelsus Clinica al Ronc

This hidden gem in Switzerland is about to become the next Mayo. The team, cancer research, diagnostic testing and health treatments are truly at the top of complementary medicine.

Strada Cantonale 158, CH-6540 Castaneda GR, alronc.ch

Plum Village

Only go if founder, Zen master Thich Nhat Hanh, is there. You know you are in the presence of someone special. There are many retreats, all based on silence, meditation, mindfulness. You leave with a new level of calm.

France, plumvillage.org

The Ashram

The owner, Cat, has made The Ashram both an oasis from the world, yet completely physically and mentally challenging. While it is based on a religious retreat (hence the name ashram), it is a full-on boot camp. Men like it and women walk out in the best shape of their lives.

Calabasas, Californina, theashram.com

EASTERN MEDICINE

WARNING
SIGNS

There is no all-knowing complementary practitioner, health guru or medical healer. We all rationally know this, but in times of intense need, as an ill and worried patient, we forget. Here are the warning signs I have picked up from my long learning curve...

This is what I tell all my friends:

If they name-drop celebrities...
find somewhere else

If they instil fear in you that if you do not do X then Y will happen...
find somewhere else

If there is a huge bouquet of fresh flowers in the waiting room...
find somewhere else

These are warning signs that they may be in it for the wrong reasons. If they were true great spiritual gurus, health pioneers, devoted eastern practitioners or even buddhist, they simply would not conduct themselves this way. I know I am making a sweeping mass generalization, but you need to keep your eyes open.

Just because someone is using the title "Dr." does not mean they have what most would assume as a complete medical school education with diploma. Even that "medical diploma" has different meanings. Do your research before trusting an integrative/complementary/eastern doctor with your health. Things are often not as they seem.

Sadly when I was extremely ill with cancer, I saw some of the worst in money-hungry so-called doctors/gurus/healers. It is as though they know your vulnerability at such a time and manipulate it. Don't turn your radar off just because you are ill and someone is making claims that you want to believe. There are many wonderful people out there, but in these largely unregulated fields there are some bad people too. Trust your gut.

Always start slow with one of their recommendations as they will almost certainly try to sell you a full program. Buy one product, one book, one more appointment. Take it slow. Make them earn your trust and money.

INDEX

Page references in *italics* indicate photographs.

// I have an 8Greens
every day //

ZAC EFRON
Actor

// The simplest way to get my greens
on the go… so easy and efficient //

KERI RUSSELL
Actress

// This is a great way of making sure
you stay healthy in a very easy
way, no matter how busy you are //

HELENA CHRISTENSEN
Supermodel

8Greens has been to The White House

// Congratulations – you have got me to drink
a green drink. I really did not find it difficult
and am now a convert to 8Greens. Thank you //

ANNA HARVEY
Director of Condé Nast, Europe and Asia

// I definitely
feel a kick
after this //

ALEX JAMES
Blur bassist

// Wow, this is good. I can taste
a hint of kale, which is good
– I know it's the real thing //

CHRISTINE D'ORNANO
Vice President, Sisley International

// Amazing deal for when I travel
or days I cannot deal with my
morning juice blender drama //

PAMELA HANSON
Fashion photographer

Dawn Russell (Lady James Russell) is a health advocate,
entrepreneur, founder of 8Greens, mother and wife.
She was named to *Vanity Fair*'s Hall of Fame, honored as one
of *Vogue*'s four women of empowerment, featured in the book
100 Most Powerful Women of the Next Generation, and was
a spokesperson for Estée Lauder who supported Russell's
foundation work. She is married to Lord James Russell,
and they live in London and New York with their two sons.

3 5 7 9 10 8 6 4 2

Preface Publishing
20 Vauxhall Bridge Road   London SW1V 2SA

Preface Publishing is part of the Penguin Random House group of companies
whose addresses can be found at global.penguinrandomhouse.com.

Penguin
Random House
UK

First published by Preface Publishing in 2017

www.penguin.co.uk

A CIP catalogue record for this book is available
from the British Library.

ISBN 978 184809 5076

Food photography by David Griffen

except pages 1, 3–13, 29, 34–35, 37, 43, 59, 66, 74, 79, 92, 96 top, 100, 131
and 142 © Dawn Russell; page 134 © iStock; page 136 © Hugo Burnand

Front cover photography by Hugo Burnand

Designed by Tim Barnes

Sources of nutritional information:
Centers for Disease Control and Prevention (CDC) July 2016
New Health Guide www.newhealthguide.org
NutritionFacts.org www.nutritionfacts.org
Organic Facts www.organicfacts.net
University of Maryland Medical Center 2011
U.S. Department of Agriculture (USDA) Nutrient Database www.ndb.nal.usda.gov/ndb

8Greens has not been evaluated by the Food and Drug Administration.
This product is not intended to diagnose, treat, cure or prevent any disease.

Printed and bound in Italy

Penguin Random House is committed to a sustainable future for our business, our readers
and our planet. This book is made from Forest Stewardship Council® certified paper.

HAVE YOU HAD SOMETHING GREEN TODAY?